NATIONAL GEOGRAPHIC

D0100645

# What Makes Me Healthy?

Nat Sui

I need good food to be healthy. Eating many kinds of foods each day helps me to be healthy.

What else do I need to be healthy?

I need water to be healthy.
Drinking lots of clean, fresh water
helps me to be healthy.

What else do I need to be healthy?

SCORP
CRAZECROSS

I need exercise to be healthy. Exercising every day helps me to be healthy.

What else do I need to be healthy?

I need sleep to be healthy. Getting lots of sleep helps me to be healthy.

What else do I need to be healthy?

I need people to care for me
to be healthy.
People who love me help me
to be healthy.

What do I need to be healthy?

I need all of these things to be healthy.

food

water

exercise

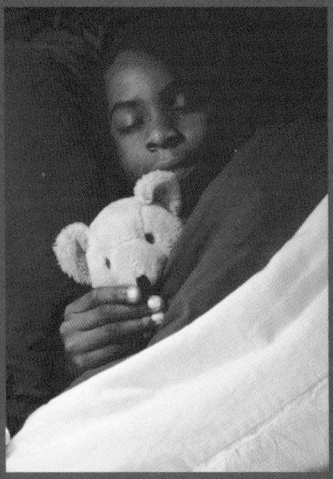

sleep

love